# The Edge of Nowhere

# The Edge of Nowhere

Reaching the Remote Kobon People
of Papua New Guinea

by
Daryl A. Schendel

Nazarene Publishing House
Kansas City, Missouri

First Printing, 1978

ISBN: 0-8341-0565-9

Printed in the
United States of America

# Contents

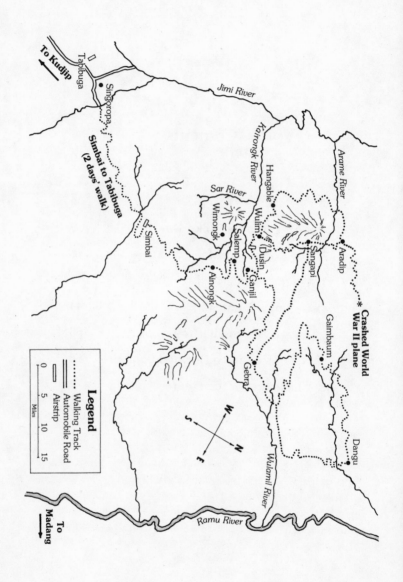

# Preface

It is the purpose of this book to try to give an insight to the development of one of the most primitive areas of the world. The Kobon people, barely contacted by the outside world 15 years ago, are struggling with the Western cultural patterns, modern civilization, and the Space Age. These ways of life are being thrust upon them at an unprecedented speed. A jump from the Stone Age to the Space Age in approximately 20 years is too much to expect from any culture, yet this is actually happening to our Kobon people; and, to a lesser degree, this is happening to all of the highlands people of Papua New Guinea.

I believe the stabilizing force is the Solid Rock Christ Jesus, who can give our young people the stability that their lives need to withstand the pressures of change.

One of the influencing factors in this change is the Highlands Highway running from the coastal towns of Lae and Madang to the highlands towns of Goroka, Mount Hagen, and Mendi. On this highway one does not encounter horses and carts, but 18-wheel tractor/trailer semi trucks moving at speeds up to 60 MPH, carrying tons and tons of cargo. Boeing 747 jets landing in Port Moresby, our capital city, along with smaller jets, link almost every population center and island of Papua New Guinea.

We have tried in these few pages to reconstruct the eight years of our lives that pertains to the Kobon people. Elizabeth and I take no credit for the work done among the Kobon people. We feel we have been an instrument that God has used in the furtherance of His kingdom. All that was done was for Jesus' sake and no other. We feel as Paul the apostle did when he wrote in Rom. 10:12-15 (NIV):

> There is no difference between Jew and Gentile—the same Lord is Lord of all and richly blesses all who call on him, for, "Everyone who calls on the name of the Lord will be saved."
> How, then, can they call on the one they have not believed in? And how can they believe in the one of whom they have not heard? And how can they hear without someone preaching to them? And how can they preach unless they are sent?

We commit this book to God in the hope that missions will come alive to those who read it.

◆　◆　◆

I am grateful to Rev. Wallace White for his help in providing information about the very beginning stages of the development of the Kobon area, and for material contained in the many patrol reports written by the missionary staff.

To my wife, Elizabeth, for her help in the preparation of this manuscript; and to my children, Susan and Daryl, Jr., who never complained about many of the hardships they had to endure because their mom and dad had a call to the primitive Kobon people.

—DARYL A. SCHENDEL

# 1

# A Trek into the Unknown

It was a typical day in the Bismark Schrader Range mountains of Papua New Guinea. The clouds seem to come from nowhere and build up into gigantic thunderheads about to burst with precipitation. Then suddenly it happened. The heavens opened in full fury on those first three patrol officers, sent out by the Australian government on an extended patrol (a trek across country). Their assignment was to take the first census and explore for the first time this extremely primitive section of the world. The year was 1955.

As the men moved farther into the Bismark Schrader Range of the then Western Highlands District, they found more tribes of people whom nobody knew even existed. In valley after valley the "explorers" discovered more groups of primitive people, who would be known later as the Kobon people.

In those early days the primitive tribes didn't live in villages, but in small family groups. When the government men came upon one of these groupings of people, they set up camp nearby and then visited the family. They would appoint a man of the tribe who appeared to have leadership ability as a government representative of their tribe. These newly appointed men were known as *Tultuls* and *Luluais*. At the same time the name of each individual in the tribe was recorded in a census book which was left with the newly appointed tribal leaders.

In those days of first contact with the outside world, these primitive people were very frightened and were reluctant to come out of hiding to have their names put in the government census book. It was mainly the young warriors, with their hand-carved bows and arrows and sharp axes, who came out to meet the strange white men.

A story is told of these early contacts, in which the Australian patrol officer and his indigenous police companion would have the people bring one of their pigs. The patrol officer would lecture the people on the power of the shotgun which he held. This of course was done through an interpreter. After much explanation the patrol officer took aim and shot the pig.

This experience was indelibly marked in the minds of these primitive people. The concept that a long tube like a bamboo pole could make such a shattering noise and the pig fall over dead was beyond their capability of understanding.

Because the patrol officer had so many kinds of magic, his every word was obeyed. Whatever he said they ran to do. Fear and respect for the law was carved into their minds for the remainder of their lives.

After this initial three-month extended exploration and registration by these patrol officers, they returned to Tabibuga, the Jimi River Government Patrol Station, and submitted their findings and discoveries to their superiors.

In 1959 the Nazarene missionaries were praying and seeking God's guidance for an outreach ministry for Rev. William Bromley. They had a conference with Mr.

Max Flavel of the Missionary Aviation Fellowship (Australian branch) in which they discussed different areas where the gospel had not been taken. Mr. Flavel suggested two areas, Simbai and Tabibuga.

After much prayer and discussion the missionaries decided to explore these two possibilities. In December, 1959, Rev. Max Conder, Rev. Wallace White, and Rev. William Bromley flew into the Simbai Government Patrol Station where they gathered information about the Simbai area.

Upon arrival at Simbai they found the Anglican Church had already begun work in the area. This was the influencing factor which caused the scouting team to look in the direction of Tabibuga, a 15-minute flight from Simbai. At Tabibuga they found that there were no other missions working in the Jimi River/Tabibuga area.

After prayer and another staff meeting, the Nazarene Mission decided to pursue the possibilities of evangelizing the thousands of people in the Jimi Valley.

While Max Conder, Wallace White, and William Bromley were at Simbai they heard about the Kobon people from an Anglican priest. There was very little known about the Kobon people who lived about a two days' walk from Simbai.

It was in 1961 when Wallace White was flying with Missionary Aviation Fellowship (MAF) pilot Max Flavel from Banz to Wewak that Mr. Flavel showed Wallace the five Kobon valleys with no means of hearing the gospel. The people in these valleys had been contacted only a couple of times by government officials.

The burden for these people weighed heavily on White and others of the missionary staff. This concern launched a volume of prayer, and plans for evangelizing these tribes of people who had never heard that there is a

God who loves them and wants them to enter into eternal life with Him.

Who would be responsible for these people? Was the Church of the Nazarene now responsible? Had God laid this outreach on the hearts of the mission staff for evangelism, or was it just for an adventure? The mission staff felt it was the responsibility of the Church of the Nazarene and that God had laid these people on their hearts, and that God would send the money and staff to do it. Surveys were made by aircraft in which houses were counted and the population estimated. This was done before the first missionaries ever made contact with the Kobon people.

The story is told by James Sambal, one of our outstanding Christian laymen of the Kobon area, about the first time a plane came over his valley at a low altitude. He recalls that he and his family were walking along a trail when they heard a very loud and strange noise in the sky. They squinted their eyes to see where the sound was coming from. As the noise came closer they saw a speck in the sky but thought it was just a bird.

Standing and watching it, the "bird" became larger and its noise got louder. Finally they could see and hear the huge yellow object very plainly. They knew for sure this monster had come out of the spirit world to kill and eat them. They all dove for the nearest foliage for hiding and peeked through the leaves as the huge monster shot past and disappeared. Sambal said they were unable to explain this intrusion from the spirit world but surmised the spirits were hungry for pig, so as soon as possible they sacrificed a pig. Sambal laughs about it now, but at that time it was a terrifying experience. No doubt the yellow "bird" was an MAF plane on a survey of the Kobon valleys.

The missionaries felt that God had opened the door

to the evangelization of these primitive people. They weren't sure just how to handle it, but knew that God had laid these people on their hearts.

Wallace White decided that he and William Bromley would make a trek or patrol for initial contact with these people, and to assess the whole situation. They would decide whether they should send a missionary family to work and live among these people or not.

During the weeks prior to February 3, 1964, White and Bromley prepared to go into the Arame River Valley and make initial contact with the Kobon people. The

*Men carrying cargo on patrol*

only information they had was from the Jimi River Patrol Officer's report and from the Anglican priest at Simbai. Actually there was very little information available because the government had been into the area but once or twice.

The men prepared for the unknown. Their supplies included a radio transceiver, 12-v. battery, tent, sleeping bags, pots and pans, a few dishes, trade items (such as matches, soap, rice, fish, and knives), salt with which to purchase food, plus a whole lot of love, faith, and courage to befriend those who had never heard of Jesus.

These missionaries knew very little about the people they were to encounter. Were they savages? Were they cannibals? Were they friendly? Would they be afraid? The answers to these questions were left in the hands of God.

As Wallace and Will prepared to go into an uncharted region and meet people who were totally untouched by the outside world, the mission staff prayed that those whom the men encountered would be receptive, and that the gospel soon would be preached to them. It was an exciting step of faith for the two missionaries as they departed family and friends.

Missionary Aviation Fellowship picked up Wallace White and all of the food and other cargo at Banz which is four miles across the Waghi Valley from Kudjip. The MAF Cessna 185 winged its way straight through the clouds to Tabibuga airstrip. Tabibuga, a 12-minute flight or two-day walk from Banz, is a small government airstrip in the Jimi Valley, the next large valley north of the Waghi Valley. The strip is about 1,400 feet long and 100 feet wide. As one approaches the strip he wonders if he will actually land on it and stop before hitting the mountain at the far end. But with much practice, skill, and

God's help, MAF pilots are able to accomplish the almost impossible.

Wallace and his pilot landed on the small grass strip and taxied in to find Will Bromley, with his cargo, ready and excited about going. The first problem, and not to be the last, was that there was too much cargo aboard. The plane could not lift off the ground. A decision was made to leave the cartons of fish and meat along with the bags of rice. The pilot was finally satisfied with 947 pounds of cargo, and away they went toward their target, another small strip called Simbai.

This too is a government airstrip, but it is not hewn out of the mountain like the one at Tabibuga. This landing strip was built on the floor of a small valley through which flows the meandering Simbai River. Valley elevation is about 5,500 feet, but the mountains on all sides go up to between 8,000 and 10,000 feet. The airstrip is situated so that an approach is made by following the Simbai River around the corner of a mountain. On beginning the final approach, one still is not in view of the airstrip. Then as the aircraft turns the corner around the mountain, the landing target appears for the first time. At the time Wallace and Will went into Simbai, the strip was 2,000 feet long, which is quite short. The valley is so small that there is no chance for a second chance with a full plane load. But they made it!

# 2

# The Kobon Patrols

Wallace White and Will Bromley arrived at Simbai safely and unloaded their cargo from the small plane. Some carriers, whom Wallace and Will had sent walking by trail from Kudjip five days earlier, also arrived. As soon as the group was all together at Simbai the clouds opened up and dumped rain in full force, making it very difficult to get organized.

A quote from Wallace and Will's patrol report reads, "We have chosen to follow the upper track. Recent fighting and trouble are reported on the Sar Valley track. Four or five killings in the past three months."

Moving into an area that experienced very little government control was nerve-racking, but God had called them to go into all the world to preach the gospel. They were to step out on faith this day, at whatever the cost might be. The men felt they must go to these people who were God's creation and as yet had never heard of Him.

The following is a complete patrol report of the first contact with the Kobon people on the *edge of nowhere,* written by Rev. Wallace White.

## From Wallace White's Report

**February 4, 1964.** Began preparations at 5 a.m. Kudjip carriers arrived at 5 a.m. Simbai carriers arrived at 7 a.m. Began walking at 7:20 a.m. Boys from Tabibuga and Kudjip showing strain. Took on seven more carriers. Plan to arrive at Salemp at 2 p.m. Road and track good to Ainongk [village], where it became bush track. Radio contact made at 9:45 a.m. with PV and LK [Kudjip and Bible College stations]. Arrived at Sangavak [village] rest house at 2 p.m. Salemp [village] in sight. Decided to remain at Sangavak. Food and firewood available. People very friendly. Signed on six new carriers for entire trip. We are at the end of the Kairongk Valley. Tomorrow we begin to climb to 6,000 feet in altitude. Wulim [village] rest house should be there. This is the last outpost. The end of the track.

**February 5, 1964.** Broke camp at 7 a.m. Terrain very rugged and steep. Descended to Kairongk River where it turns toward the Jimi River. . . . Radio contact made with PV and LK and HG at 9:45 a.m. Noticed a white object on distant mountain in the direction of our travel. The interpreter said it was a signal for distant groups to come for a visit. . . . Continued walking up. Steady climb until Wulim was reached at 3:30 p.m. The carriers had an extremely difficult time today. Water and mud in half the areas traveled through. Leeches were discovered in the campsite at Wulim. The Kudjip and Tabibuga boys loathed them and screamed when they were found on their legs. The campsite is in very poor condition. Built by the last patrol [government]. Some food was brought in by local people. Not enough to feed the boys we have with us. . . . The houses are much better built than those encountered along the Kairongk Valley. They have

17

karuka leaf [pandanus leaf] roofs with split plank vertical sides. Tall enough to walk into and out of. . . . We sighted only three women today. The local population is very sparse. Eight and one-half hours walking today. Camp altitude approximately 6,600-7,000 feet. Sleeping in the tent tonight for protection from the leeches. Radio contact at 3:30 p.m. . . . Wulim is much farther from Salemp than is shown on the map.


**February 6, 1964.** Rained all night. Bugs are very bad. The biting kind. Unable to break camp as yet on account of rain, 7:50 a.m. Two cases of malaria among Kudjip boys. Gwola has a bad cold. Made radio contact with PW [Jimi station] only at 9:45 a.m. Decided to check cargo and rest today. Will continue trip tomorrow. . . . Talked with several of the local people. Most of the population are away at Sangapi. Didn't learn much about the customs and language.


**February 7, 1964.** No rain during night. Broke camp at 6:50 a.m. Traveled up to ridge and pass for one hour. The bush is full of leeches. Traveled at fast pace, arriving at Sangapi [village] at 1 p.m. No radio contact made in morning. Unable to extend aerial. Last Patrol left a rest house. Rest house still in good condition. . . . Encountered some of local population. Women fled and men sang out [called out] warning others of our approach. We learned of their fashion of shaking hands. You crook the index finger of the person being greeted. A jerk downward should produce a pop or click. This brought a good deal of laughing from the people. Some food and firewood were brought in by the locals around Sangapi. . . . We saw, in all, about 25 people from the immediate area today. . . . The last five miles today were very painful. I

18

sprained or pulled my leg. I managed with two sticks. We trust the leg will be well enough to travel in two or three days.

**February 8, 1964.** Only two or three people came into camp this morning. We have sung [called] out for the boss boy twice. 10:30 a.m. No sign of the local population. Boss boy has not arrived. . . . 10:45 a.m. Boss boy arrived. We discussed cargo stored by Mark Sage [government patrol officer] on December patrol. "We did not open the building until you arrived," it was explained. His reply was, "That's good. I worked poison when I closed the building. You did the good thing." . . . It was agreed that the people would meet on Monday to discuss the airstrip building and station. . . . Food was brought in today. A promise to bring plenty tomorrow.

**February 9, 1964.** Sunday. Services held at 11 a.m. Interpreters used on this trip were Gii [Gee] from Kairongk [village] and Duwaren [Doo-*wa*-ren] from Sangavak [village]. This boy Duwaren is able to interpret all the way into the Arame Valley and Sangapi. . . . Visited a house at the foot of the strip. I feel that the people are afraid of us. . . . One of the houses of the area is located at the bottom of the proposed airstrip site. On this our third day in the area, we decided to visit and see what contact could be established. We found several people in the house who had not been up to the campsite. We entered the house and talked with the men there. There were four men from Wulim and four men living in the house. Two small boys were present. One baby and two women. We were permitted to go only into the area where the men stay. The men explained that, should we see into their rooms, when we left, they would die. I moved toward the hallway and they objected. . . . They had hidden their weapons when we approached the house. I persuaded them to bring them out so we could see them. One by one, they all brought them out for inspection. They were lethal and in good order. . . .

When we were preparing to return, one of the boys called my attention to a clump of tankets. In the top of the clump was a skull of a young boy. The body was buried beneath the ground, and the head was displayed above the ground. . . . I took out a flashlight while sitting by the fire and talking. When I turned it on, they leaped to stay clear of the beam as though it were a knife. . . . Matches are a marvel to them. They burn their hands with them. Therefore, they are afraid to use them. . . . We are seeing some yaws and skin diseases. On the whole the people appear to be healthy.

**February 10, 1964.** Monday. Work on the rest house was commenced. Roofs repaired and other things were

*The rest house at Sangapi*

20

straightened. 9:45 a.m. We attempted radio contact. Unable to raise any of our stations. . . . some men and boys came into camp this morning. We took a word list and discussed customs. Everything appeared friendly. . . . We took down names of the rivers and creeks nearby. . . . People from four of the boss boy's houses came bringing food. Plenty of it. All together about 70 [people]. This means an average of 17½ people per house. We feel that it will be alright to begin the return trip tomorrow.

**February 11, 1964.** Broke camp at 6:50 a.m. Reached Wulim campsite at 11:45 a.m. Decided to continue to Kairongk River. Unable to continue. Camped on the track at Homun River. Made radio contact at 3:30 p.m. Hope to make Simbai tomorrow. Radio contact at 7 p.m. . . . We learned the Kiap [government patrol officer] from Simbai is at the rest house at Salemp. It seems a murder was committed when we passed through there last week. . . . We camped here on the track. During the night a person came along the track. The carriers thought immediately that he was a poison man [something like a witch doctor]. They wanted to kill him. This is the way trouble begins.

**February 12, 1964.** Rain started at 1 a.m. and continues at the present, 7:30 a.m. Unable to break camp. 8:30 a.m., rain slacked off. 9 a.m., broke camp and proceeded to the point Ambonek River joins the Kairongk River. Because of rain the rivers were in flood. Travelling miserable. Unable to cross the Ambonek River. Built bridge. Completed crossing at 1:30 p.m. Proceeded to Womuk [village]. Arrived at 3:30 p.m.

**February 13, 1964.** Broke camp at 6:30 a.m. and proceeded to Simbai. Arrived at 9:45 a.m. Expecting MAF plane at 3 p.m. Plane unable to land due to weather. It returned to Banz.

**February 14, 1964.** Plane arrived at 10:15 a.m. Departed from Tabibuga at 10:35 a.m.

*Respectfully submitted,*
Wallace White.


September 28, 1964, the second patrol was made by Will Bromley and Lee Eby. As we have just read, an area in the Arame Valley known as "Sangapi" was decided on as the place to build an airstrip and the mission station. As yet there was no missionary to send and very little money to build with but God provides. These were His people who had gone astray. He wanted them to have a chance to hear that Jesus has come as the Supreme Sacrifice. They no longer have to kill animals to make themselves righteous or to placate the evil spirits.

Will and Lee went into Sangapi with the purpose of contacting the people again, and also mark out some ground for an airstrip and mission station.

From this particular report came the title of this book. On October 1, 1964, Lee Eby stood at the Salemp village where the road, approximately 2 feet to 4 feet wide and practically straight up and straight down in some places, ends. A grass-roofed and reed-walled house, which is used sometimes as a rest house by the government patrol officers, is situated on the top of a ridge which protrudes out into the Kairongk Valley. At this most spectacular spot Lee stood looking out across the valley and on to the tops of the mountains and said, "The good road ends at Salemp—the edge of nowhere."

It was on this same patrol that on Sunday morning they had made breakfast tea (Will was an Englishman and he loved his morning tea). As they were cleaning things up after eating, they glanced into the drum of drinking water and found a rat floating on the water. They had a good laugh over it hoping they had boiled the water enough when they had prepared tea for breakfast.

June 22, 1965. The third patrol was made into the Arame Valley by Lee Eby and Bruce Blowers. They spent about 13 days among these people, which produced some interesting experiences and insights. During this reconaissance patrol the people seemed much less afraid and began to come and take a closer look at the strange white people.

Lee and Bruce, having first spent a few days at Sangapi, went on down the Arame River. In this new area they found people who seemed to decorate themselves much more than the Sangapi people. They also found that the people in this area spoke a different language. It took three interpreters to talk to them.

The pig houses along the trail looked like small horse stalls. Each little pig house was divided into stalls just large enough to accommodate one pig.

On this patrol the people responded excitedly when told that a missionary family was going to come to live in their valley.

The fourth patrol was into still another area to contact other tribal groups of the Kobon language. This patrol went into the Gebra Valley. It is a beautiful area with a view that can hardly be matched anywhere in the world. On a clear day, which is not often, one can see all the way out to the ocean to a volcanic island that often has smoke or steam coming from it. Between the ocean and the Gebra Valley is the meandering Ramu River with vast areas of dark snake- and crocodile-infested jungles.

On this patrol Wallace White and Ray Bolerjack were privileged to make initial contact with a tribal group that probably numbers around 1,000.

Wallace and Ray had been taken to Gebra Valley via the long way around by a couple of local guides. The guides had their reasons for not taking the shortest route. Most of the time such routing has to do with the evil spirit called the "Konjuki." He is the most fierce of all the evil spirits and he is always in the high mountain jungles. The people don't like to take any chances going into certain areas, especially with a couple of white-skinned strangers.

After walking for 12 hours over some of the most rugged country in the world, Wallace and Ray arrived at Gebra rest house. The government patrol officer, with a contingent of police, were leaving with five prisoners. There had just been two women murdered in the area and they were there to investigate and apprehend those who had committed the crime.

The first night Wallace and Ray were at Gebra they had their carriers call out for food to be brought in by the local people. This custom of "calling out" is the means of communication among the Kobon people. If a person needs something or someone they stand on a ridge, fill their lungs with air and let loose with a bloodcurdling yodel. If the distance is too great, someone picks up the message and passes it on with the same type of yodel.

During the first night everything was quiet. As the evening wore on, all of a sudden a score of men and boys started stomping their feet and yodeling and running back and forth just outside the grass hut where the two missionaries were staying. Wallace confesses that both he and Ray thought they were going to be killed. But as it turned out these men had been excited that these missionaries had come to their valley. The local men had answered "the call" and had brought them food. Wallace and Ray were quite relieved when they realized this was a friendly gesture and went out and greeted these men with a broad smile of thanksgiving.

The fifth patrol into Sangapi and the Arame Valley

was a different kind of patrol. Rev. Bruce Blowers, his wife, Ruth, and two of their four children, David and Darlene, went to these people on a mission of love. They were anxious to get construction started on the airstrip as well as to work on the language. Not least of their concerns, they wanted to tell these people that Jesus loves them. Their visit was planned to last 24 days, from June 21 to July 14, 1966.

It was a long and slow trek for Ruth and the twins. The route took them over mountain passes and through deep valleys; through rain, and under the scorching sun. It took eight days of walking to reach Sangapi, their intended destination.

As camp was set up at Sangapi, Bruce immediately organized the carriers and local people for cutting grass and making the bush house livable. This latter task including chasing out the resident rats which was pretty successful, except at night, when the house belongs to them.

Bruce was able to start a group of people working on the proposed airstrip site while he struggled with the preparation of a word list for a simple Kobon dictionary. He didn't have an interpreter who knew Pidgin English very well, so he had to do most of the word gathering by pointing to different objects.

After a few days at Sangapi MAF did an air drop of supplies. This was a very frightening experience for the local people. They had no idea where the aircraft had come from, so were sure that the spirits had sent it. Much of the cargo was soap, oil for cooking, shovel heads, axes, machetes, dishpans for carrying dirt, eggs (of which only two survived intact), mail, cinnamon rolls from the missionaries at Kudjip, and other things.

The day finally arrived when the Blowers had to say good-by to their newly adopted people. They preached

25

to them for the last time. The twins, David and Darlene, were ready to stay there permanently, but they too had to say good-by to their new friends. Ahead of them was the long trek back to the Simbai government patrol station and the MAF plane which would take them back to their work in the Waghi valley.

Another reconnoiter patrol followed Bruce and Ruth Blower's trip within a couple of weeks. It was important to keep the work moving on the construction of the air-strip. Wallace White and Ken Dodd made this patrol. Dodd had come over to Papua New Guinea to build the hospital at Kudjip. This patrol found but a few people working on the Sangapi airstrip. Upon the arrival of the missionaries, quite a number of local people came to help. Wallace and Ken spent about 17 days and were able to keep the construction program going.

One of the often stated comments on almost all patrols was that there were not many people to be seen but everyone felt that there were more people back in the bush. The missionaries felt that people were too afraid to let themselves be seen.

October, 1966, was a greatly anticipated month in the lives of the Daryl Schendels. It was the fulfillment of God's call. We arrived in Papua New Guinea as a very enthusiastic family. Susan, age five, and Daryl, Jr., age two, were wide-eyed and trying to take in everything. It was all so strange to them: the missionary family, the local people, the funny language called Pidgin English, and the local customs. Elizabeth and I too were trying to absorb everything around us. I remember well Bruce Blowers taking me up into the bush that first day to see a "sing-sing" (the local festival dance). I couldn't believe my eyes. I asked myself, Am I really here, or is this a dream?

In December, 1966, we went to Brisbane, Australia, to complete a course on linguistics given by the Summer

Institute of Linguistics (Wycliff Bible Translators). It was the consensus of the Mission Council that if we were going into the Kobon area we would need to work on the unwritten Kobon language. We needed this linguistics training.

Upon completion of the course in the middle of February, 1967, we returned to Kudjip. We began immediate plans for my first patrol to the Kobon people. On February 28, 1967, I made my first patrol, scheduled to last until March 13, 1967. Also on this trip was Ray Bolerjack, leader of the patrol, and Marcus Dawson, who was with the Wycliff Bible Translators. Our goal was to make contact with the people at Salemp and Gebra, to check on how the work was progressing at the airstrip site at Sangapi, and try to assess the population centers. I will never forget the day we left the road at Salemp on our way to Gebra; we had to chop our way through the thick rain forest and move almost straight up the mountain to a pass that was about 8,000 feet high. We were also occupied with picking leeches from our legs and the carriers' legs. I remember looking at Ray, who was breathing very hard with perspiration running down his face; he said, "I would only do this for Jesus' sake." I felt the same way.

Later on in the day, about noon, it started to pour buckets of rain. It continued all afternoon. Packs on the poles the carriers were carrying started coming apart, and everything was soaked through. We had to drop into a river and walk knee deep in some areas for about 2 miles and then just head out through the jungle. I never did see a trail of any sort when we left the river.

About 6:15 p.m., Ray and I arrived at the rest house at Gebra. The carriers were spread out all along the trail behind us. Marcus Dawson found a local house and spent a most miserable night sitting up, for there wasn't enough room for him and all the carriers to lie down and sleep. He and the carriers made it to the Gebra rest house the next day about 9 a.m., exhausted.

We moved on to Sangapi a couple of days later. We did not find the numbers of people in Gebra-Sangapi valleys as was originally estimated. First estimates were about 5,000 people. As we moved through heavy jungles on our way to Sangapi and the proposed airstrip and mission station, we came upon a group of people in their gardens. One of the men had a finger from his dead wife hanging around his neck. This was to show her spirit that he was mourning for her so she would not cause him any harm. He was afraid that she would cause some injury or illness to come upon him.

We arrived at Sangapi. Not much work was being done on the airstrip. While we were camped at Sangapi we were told that each family group had several large houses scattered around the area. When we discovered this, we knew that the population in the Gebra and Sangapi valleys was not anyway near the original estimations.

When we finished our patrol we reevaluated the building of the airstrip and mission station at Sangapi. We tentatively decided to look for another airstrip and mission station site in a more centrally located place in the Kairongk Valley.

Because we did not relocate to the Kobon area as soon as anticipated, I went on several more patrols. On every trip it became clearer that we should move our sights to the Salemp village of the Kairongk Valley.

On a patrol with Dr. Glen Irwin and Neville Bartle on April 8, 1969, we went into the Gebra Valley to contact the people again. While there we observed the method used by the Kobons to bury their dead. It is most unusual. When a person dies or is killed the body is placed in the main living area of the house on a small platform about two or three feet off the ground. The corpse's legs are placed over a pole at the knees and is left there for three or four days. During this time people from all over the area come to mourn.

They rub mud all over their bodies including face and hair, and as they approach the house of the deceased they begin to wail. They move into the house and stand by the body still wailing. When someone new comes, the family begins to wail also. Then they will eat and talk and

*The burial of the Kobon dead is on a platform with a picket fence around it, placed about 50 feet from the house.*

have a social occasion. The intensity of the "cry" or mourning depends on the social status of the person who has died. The most intense mourning is for a young man of the tribe who would have become one of their warriors had he lived.

When everyone that the family considers important has viewed the body and mourned, and they have eaten together, the family takes the small platform and body about 50 feet from the house and puts a rough stake fence around it. They will put some of the deceased's personal belongings on the fence to be used on his journey to the other world. A pig, sweet potatoes, and taro are cooked near the body so he won't be hungry while he is on this long journey.

The remains stay exposed on the platform until the bones are bare. The bones are then buried, but the skull is left and put into the house. After 10 years, pigs are killed and the skull is placed in a very large tree deep in the rain forest. This usually terminates any further placation of the person's spirit.

One story is told about a poison man whom the family had hired to talk to the deceased. While the bones were still on the platform the poison man placed a reed through the jaw bone and asked some questions. The movement of the jaw bone up and down on the reed was how the dead man responded to the family's questions.

# 3

# On the Honda Trail

In February, 1969, the Papua New Guinea Interim Council of the Church of the Nazarene set January, 1970, as the target date when we were to set up a mission station at Salemp Village in the Kairongk Valley. Elizabeth, who was involved at the mission hospital at Kudjip, and I had to be relieved of our responsibilities. Gradually they had to be given to someone else. This was surely a step of faith for all of us on the field. But for the Schendel family, Elizabeth, Susan, Daryl, Jr., and me, it was the realization of why we came to Papua New Guinea in 1966.

Two responsibilities were immediately before us; construction of a workshop and missionary residence, and hiring men to carry our supplies in to the location.

It was July 28, 1969, that I made my first trip in to Salemp to initiate our evangelistic thrust on the edge of nowhere. I arrived at Simbai via Missionary Aviation Fellowship with just a part of my cargo. The plane had to return for my Honda 90 trail motorbike. The road is a walking trail, but for the sake of time the bike is more practical. At one stage there were, by actual count, 125 bridges on one 20-mile stretch of the trail (The road was mostly clay, which, when it rained, became like grease. To keep the bike upright was a major task). About 100 of these smaller bridges consisted of two logs 6 to 8 inches in diameter laid across a stream. On these logs are placed split branches. These branches are tied down by bush rope which is found nearby growing along the ground. The rope is quite strong for a few months, but the tropical sun and the almost daily rains have a way of rotting it.

The approach to these bridges is anything but smooth. The logs, sitting on the banks raise the structure 6 to 8 inches higher than the ground. So when the front wheel of the motorbike hits one side of the bridge and the rope breaks (which happens often) all the split branches bunch up at the opposite end of the bridge and the motorbike finds itself at the bottom of the stream, with the rider draped over the handle bars.

After a while, I was able to lift the front wheel up on

*When there is no bridge the motorbike must be carried across the stream.*

the bridge and coast across to the other side and then give it gas on the way down off of the bridge. At most of the bridges the approach is about a 45° angle descent and then up the same angle on the other side. No brakes or throttle can be used on the bridges. I had to find the best way of crossing a bridge through trial and error.

It was a nice sunny afternoon when Wallace White and A. A. E. Berg, superintendent of the Australian District, became a classic illustration of bridge mishaps. The two men were riding tandem on their way into Salemp. As they were crossing a small log and limb bridge, the top surface of the structure cascaded beneath them. The motorbike ended up in the stream below. Wallace was hanging on one long runner of the bridge and Rev. Berg on the other. A bit surprised and bruised they managed to extricate themselves from the precarious position and start the process of retrieving their motorbike. They eventually arrived in Salemp.

Meanwhile, back to our move to Salemp. When I went in to build the workshop I had a difficult time finding enough carriers to transport all the supplies into Salemp to complete both workshop and house. I took two helpers with me from Kudjip, so it was necessary to supply them with materials. I designed a box for the back of my motorbike, which was the source of many sprawling accidents.

I remember one in particular where the motorbike, cargo, and I were spread all over the road and bridge. It was a section of road made up mainly of slate rock which became very slippery in the rain. The stretch of road in question was on the side of a mountain. The terrain on one side was 500 feet straight down, on the other side it was straight up. Because the road had been hewn out of the side of the mountain, it became steeper as it went along the side of this mountain. Part way up the mountain there was a bridge at a left turn in the road. The bridge itself was not level but on an angle. It also had a 6-inch jump to get up onto it. The road ascended sharply on the other side so there was no chance to coast while on the bridge. It was full throttle all the way. Coming to the bridge I jumped the front wheel up onto the logs, but the wheel slipped to the right and in a twinkling of an eye I was standing with my feet in the creek bed on the downhill side, holding on to the motorbike above me, trying to keep it from going on down the mountain. The cargo from the box was scattered everywhere.

I murmured, "Now Lord, just how am I going to get out of this one without the motorbike going to the bottom of the ravine?" My answer came; as I tried to ease the bike down I discovered it was caught on the bridge above me on a small stick. With an understated, but sincere "Thank You, Lord!" I climbed up onto the road, bruised and scratched but not injured seriously, and started the task of gathering up the cargo and getting on my way again.

It was a thrill to be able to start the Salemp church at the same time I began the workshop construction. It was exciting to gather a group of 30 people who had never heard the good news of Jesus Christ. What an experience to look into the dirty, leathery faces of people who had never known of soap, but wanting to understand what Christianity is all about. To be able to tell them of a God who loves them and wants to look out for them and be their Loving Companion and Savior was a real thrill. This was a concept so foreign to them that at first they were unable to comprehend that kind of God.

For most of the people in church that day it was a first time to attempt to pray. I told them to bow their heads and close their eyes, but they were not sure what I was going to do to them while they weren't looking.

Most of them bowed their heads but in no way would they close their eyes. Later I was told they didn't want me to steal their pigs or women while they weren't looking.

We had brought a crew into Salemp to cut planks from trees felled up in the rain forest.

The process of cutting planks is a long one. First the right kind of tree must be found; it can't be too hard or too soft. The trees have to be located in the correct place on the side of the mountain. Trees are cut by axe or a crosscut saw.

After felling, the tree is cut into 10- to 15-foot lengths and rolled onto a platform of runners extended out from the side of the mountain. The tree is marked for cutting into planks with a string covered with the carbon that comes inside flashlight batteries. The cutting process involves one man who gets under the platform and another on top. The two of them saw the log into a semblance of a plank. The 1" x 6" plank may vary from ½ inch to 1½ inches thick and from 4 to 8 inches wide.

The crew eventually carried the newly sawed boards down the mountain to our house site.

The irony of the procedure was that the crew I flew in had very little understanding of the art of plank cutting, even though they assured me they were experienced. I eventually had to obtain another crew who at least had some idea of the skill involved.

The workshop at Salemp was a small building constructed out of trees cut up in the rain forest about 2 miles from the mission station. These 3- to 6-inch by 30-foot trees were stripped of their bark and carried on men's shoulders to the workshop location. The ground was leveled and we started construction of our first building. Some of the local people sat around and watched while others pitched in and helped with the building. This was the realization of hopes and prayers initiated in

1964 by Wallace White, William Bromley, and the rest of the missionary staff.

I had the workshop fairly well finished and gradually got all equipment for the workshop from Simbai when it was time to return to the Waghi Valley via Simbai to pick up my responsibilities there for a few more months.

On September 22, 1969, having been relieved at Kudjip in the Waghi Valley for a month or so, I went back to Salemp to begin building our home. I left from the Kudjip airstrip via MAF plane in the morning and arrived at Salemp at 3 p.m. after a two-hour ride on a motorbike. The men I brought in to help with the construction arrived on foot about 8 p.m.

We were not able to use cement because of the high cost of air freight. Obtaining gravel and sand at the river, about a 45-minute walk down and 1½-hours' walk back up, really made the use of cement prohibitive in both money and time.

It was necessary for us to obtain some wood which we called ironwood. It is lumber that can be left in the ground for about 10 years after it has been cut.

We had to obtain 20 young men from an adjoining valley to carry our cargo in from Simbai because the local men were involved in the "sing-sing" festivals. In a week's time we had cut enough ironwood to start putting in the foundation posts. We also had a crew up in the rain forest cutting round poles for the framework.

Our cargo destined for Salemp included a prized possession, a 3,000-watt gasoline generator that we had purchased in the United States and brought with us to Papua New Guinea. I disassembled the mechanism and put it into the Cessna 206 for a trip to a place where the sun and fire were the only source of warmth and illumination. When it arrived in Salemp by carriers, the Lord gave me the know-how to put it all back together again, and in running condition. We thanked the Lord more than once for the power that that generator provided.

An incident with the generator was quite amusing. The engine was a battery start model and I had it rigged up in the house on a remote start and stop. One day four boys from way out beyond our settlement came in to see the white people at Salemp. I saw the young men standing at the door of the workshop looking at everything. In our house, I stepped over to the remote start switch and flipped the generator on. The generator was located just inside of the workshop. When that generator kicked over I've never seen Kobon boys move so fast. I didn't see them again for some time. Later they returned a little more cautious than before.

*The Schendels in front of the missionary home being built at Salemp.*

Our house construction moved steadily, but sometimes slowly. Some planks finally came in and I was able to put them on the floor of the kitchen. The rest of the house had woven bamboo for a floor covering because we had neither the time nor the money for the whole house to be floored with planks.

Let me try to explain our house. We built it mostly from local material. It was 35 x 45 feet. The foundation posts were of ironwood placed in holes about 2 feet deep and about 7 feet apart. We placed poles about 8 inches in diameter on the ironwood stumps to form the main supports. As previously stated, the poles are roughly cut trees, small at one end, big at the other, and nearly as straight as a dog's hind leg. Across these bearers were placed more poles of 4-inch diameter—more or less—placed about a foot apart. On these floor joists we placed split pieces of the trunk of a pandanus tree. These were nailed down, with two layers of split woven bamboo placed on the top of the pandanus strips. As you can imagine, the floor is quite solid, although when Elizabeth swept the floor the dust filtered down through the woven bamboo.

The studs were made from tree poles, as well as the top and bottom plates and gables and rafters. All parts of the house were made from round poles except window and door frames and the kitchen floor. The corrugated iron which was used for the roof had been flown into Simbai and carried by hand the 20 miles to the location of the house at Salemp.

Woven reed matting was placed on the walls over an aluminium-coated tar paper. We had no ceiling; the walls were 7 feet high. Our home had three bedrooms, an office, bathroom with flush toilet and bucket shower, pantry, kitchen, living room, front and back porch.

It took us one month to get the house under a roof;

it seemed to have rained every day. One afternoon when I was out with the crew cutting and removing trees I began to count rain showers. I finally quit after counting seven of them. After all, one can only get so wet, then it doesn't matter anymore.

On October 13, Elizabeth and the children, Susan and Daryl, Jr., arrived at Simbai. I went out on my motorbike and picked up the children. We were nearly halfway home when it started to pour. We got soaked and so cold we decided to stay a while in a local house. They were very excited to have white people as their guests. Our hosts gave us some sweet potatoes and started a fire to dry us out. After getting warmed up a bit we were on our way again. Elizabeth and Merna Blowers (Bruce Blowers' missionary sister) walked. It took them about 7½ hours. My family was excited to see their new home even if it was not finished.

Many people came into see the new white family. Some just wanted to touch the kids to see if the white skin would come off.

Business in Kudjip caused me to have split interests. It was necessary for me to leave our building projects more than once to care for mission concerns. In the back of my mind was the knowledge that in just a couple of months we could give Salemp our full attention.

November 25, 1969, I returned to Salemp with a Papua New Guinean carpenter. We had left workmen at the construction site working on the house matting when we had to leave and they had finished a great deal of the reed matting for the walls. We got started right away on the house, hoping to complete it. A crew of young men was again selected to carry cargo in from Simbai, and I made trips on my motorbike trying to get necessary food and supplies in. The people were very busy still with their yearly "sing-sing" festivals.

On December 1 I made a trip out to Simbai on my motorbike. On the way back I had one of the worst trail accidents I've ever experienced. It was at a bridge where a mountain landslide covered the road at one end. The people had no trouble walking over it, but I had to work it just right to make it over on the motorbike.

As I came across the bridge I had to lean over onto the handle bars to keep the front end from coming up off the ground and I had to give it full throttle. This particular time the engine coughed halfway up and died. I started backwards down onto the bridge. Then I went down very hard. My foot and leg slipped into a hole and I straight-armed the ground trying to protect myself. I tore muscles loose up in my shoulder. The pain was excruciating, so I just laid there on the bridge for some time with the motorbike over on its side. Gasoline poured out in a steady stream. After a period of time, I'm not sure just how long, I was able to pull my leg out of the hole in the bridge and get my motorbike up onto its wheels. But I was unable to move, so I just stayed there holding onto the bike. I have no idea how long I was there. All the people around the area who saw the accident thought I was dead and were afraid to help for the fear that my spirit might harm them.

The government patrol officer was out in this particular area, so the bush telegraph started "broadcasting" that the white man had killed himself on his motorbike. When the patrol officer heard this he came to my rescue on his motorbike. He gave me some aspirin and helped me get things under control enough to get me started on my way again. I had about six miles more of trail to cover, and with the Lord's help I made it safely before dark.

In the days that followed, with my arm in a sling, I was unable to work on our house. This put the house construction behind schedule a bit. But the Lord is good and I praise Him for being with me, and I am thankful for the prayers of our Nazarene family around the world. For if I had fallen off the bridge, I may not have survived.

During the first week of January, 1970, Elizabeth and I wound up our work at Kudjip. The Sidney Knox Memorial Church had a sending service for us which was a very moving experience. The national Christians, with their natural flair for symbolism, presented us with two gifts: a kerosene lantern which signified the carrying of the light of the gospel to those who have never heard, and a long bush knife or machete which represented cutting a new trail for Christ. After long speeches they put a

*The Schendel sending service at the Sidney Knox Memorial Church at Kudjip. From left to right: Wallace White; Elizabeth, Susan, Daryl, and Daryl, Jr., Schendel; James Sambal; and Pastor Yimbalk.*

ring of flowers around our family which was significant of the church's love and prayerful support as we went to those who had never heard.

January 6, 1970, finally arrived and what an exciting time we had! Our suitcases were packed and ready for a Missionary Aviation Fellowship plane. When the plane arrived at our Kudjip airstrip, all the missionary staff and many local Christians were there to give us words of encouragement and to say good-by. Our hearts were overwhelmed when we realized that prayers from around the world were in the process of being answered. We were the recipients of these answered prayers.

Climbing into the Missionary Aviation Fellowship Cessna 206, we waved a last good-bye, took off, and then began to wing our way to Simbai, just 20 miles from home. Upon arrival we all four got onto our Honda 90

*Looking down on the Salemp station*

trail motorbike (as we would do many times in the future) and headed out for Salemp and home.

As we came over the last crest on the road and looked down at our new house we said, "Thank You, Lord, for this privilege You have given to us to come to the edge of nowhere to minister to the Kobon people."

# 4

# Getting a Right Start

A congregation at Salemp was gathered together before there was a building. Our Sunday worship services were conducted out in the open in those early days. When the sun was out we thought we would be cooked. When the sun went behind the clouds we got chilled. Then came the rains and winds. It didn't take long for us to recognize that we had to obtain property to build a church on, so we could move our services inside. We were fortunate to get some ground on a ridge overlooking the Kairongk valley.

Property for the mission station had already been secured, but it is our strong conviction that the local church must be situated on its own ground, disconnected from the mission station. The reason for this is that the mission is an outside or foreign agency that is supported from outside sources. Whereas the local church must take on the full responsibility of its own upkeep. It belongs to the people.

We began building the Salemp church with only one or two local Christians. The other Koboners weren't too excited about building a church for no pay. The search

*Putting Kunai grass onto the roof of the Salemp church.*

*Then the roof collapsed!*

for materials took time, but we finally secured enough round-pole timber, so we started putting the frame together. The poles were very small but still we tried to span the building without a center post. Everything was going fine until we started to put the long "kunai" (koonaee) grass roof on. This material is very heavy when it is wet and green, so when combined with 15 or 20 men on top of the building we were in for trouble.

Almost half of the roof grass had been tied to the frame when we heard a great deal of commotion going on at the church building site. Someone called out that the roof had collapsed and one man was dead. We went running. When we arrived we found a collapsed church roof and a man injured but not dead. Some women immediately got pots of water and doused the injured workman. The group was convinced that the evil spirit who had caused the church to collapse was still around and they wanted it to leave this man alone.

We rebuilt the church, this time with a center post. If we hadn't I'm afraid nobody would have gone into it. It wasn't too long before we dedicated the Salemp Church of the Nazarene.

One problem that we faced almost immediately was the question of how or where does one start to evangelize a people who have no idea what you are talking about. Also how to keep the concepts of the gospel so simple that the interpreter, as well as the congregation, knows what you're talking about.

I believe the Holy Spirit was our Guide and helped as as we struggled with this problem. We decided that first of all the Kobons must understand who God is, what He is like, and that He is the Creator. In order for these illiterate people to understand, one must move very slowly in presenting new concepts. We spent Sunday after Sunday just with the simple story of the first two or three days

46

of creation. For almost two years we preached and taught the biblical account of creation. The Sunday school lessons covered much of the same material. We soon discovered that the children were able to move more quickly in developing an understanding of the Word than the adults.

When we felt that the Kobons were understanding the creation story fairly well, we highlighted the remainder of the Old Testament and tried to bridge it to the New Testament by explaining that Jesus was the Son of this God we had been talking about. Having tried to lay a foundation, we began to teach and preach about Jesus Christ; His relationship to God the Father, His death on the Cross, and His resurrection. From these events we presented the possibility of forgiveness of sins and eternal life.

We started another church at a place called Ganjil, about a half hour's walk from Salemp. Because there were older people there who were unable to walk to church we started an outreach ministry among them. We used the same scheme here in the presentation of the gospel. At Ganjil we sat on the ground under large banana trees. The people were eager to learn, but it too was a very slow process. Today we have a growing, organized church in that community.

We always had at least four elements of worship in our services no matter how poor or primitive the people were. These four elements were: Prayer, singing, offering, and a Bible lesson or message.

Prayer was always a new experience for our Kobon people. In those early days they were afraid we were going to do something to them while they prayed; things like stealing their women or pigs. They would usually bow their heads, but never closed their eyes.

Singing had to be taught to them. At first we sang

mainly in Pidgin English, for we didn't have any songs in the Kobon language. But very soon we developed indigenous songs, for it is very important that people worship with songs that are meaningful to them.

The offering was also an important part of their training and worship. If someday they were to support a pastor and God's work they had to learn to give, even though they were not Christians. Their offerings consisted of money as well as sweet potatoes, corn, beans, or whatever they had. We believed that if we waited until they became Christians before we told them about financial stewardship they would think we were trying to get all their money. This approach to giving has worked out well.

We didn't have an offering plate at the Ganjil church so we began to look around for something that would be suitable for this particular part of the worship service. We discovered that the red blossom of a banana tree was just the thing for it is shaped like a small bowl. So each Sunday morning we had a beautiful new offering blossom.

The Bible lessons had to be very simple. We used large Sunday school teaching pictures and homemade charts with stick-figure pictures. At first the pictures and charts were difficult for our people to understand, for they had never seen a picture before. But gradually they began to learn how to look at the pictures and charts with understanding. The truths of the Scriptures began to open up to them.

In order to evangelize the Kobon people it was important for us to understand their cultural beliefs about life and creation. Almost all people have their own teachings about these seeming mysteries. Our Kobon people are no different. They have their beliefs and stories. It was important for us to have some understanding of these so that we could relate them to the truths of the gospel.

Kobon man in "Sing-sing" attire: wide apron of bark netting; bird of paradise feathers through his nose and combined with hawk feathers in his headdress. The slender three-foot pole at the back has a lesser bird of Paradise on top. Note bongo-type drum.

The Kobons do have a group of spirits which they must appease. Nothing in their lives happens by chance. Everything has a cause. If a person stubs his toe or injures his leg on a stick, he will take the offending object with him, if possible, and conduct a certain ritual upon returning home in order to placate the spirit that caused the injury. He would believe that a spirit is trying to get his attention for some reason. The spirit is either hungry or angry at something the victim has done.

One important discovery we made was in the area of killing pigs for a sacrifice. At the yearly festivals called "sing-sings," several hundred pigs may be killed and sacrificed to the ancestral spirits. The pigs must be killed by the "poison man" or at least have been blessed by him. They are then dressed out and cooked in a certain way. The "sing-sing" pig, among our Kobon people, will always have the hair left on it, and its blood is carefully saved and made into a blood pudding. The cooking must be done ceremonially. A hole is dug in the ground and then stones are heated until they explode. After this the food is placed in the earthen oven under the direct supervision of the "poison man." Food cooked in the earth oven is called a "mumu."

When the food is removed from the earthen ovens it is proportioned out to all the invited guests. Involved in this festival are the payments of debts and trying to outdo the other tribe's "sing-sing" festival the previous year. Then the dancing starts. It usually begins late in the afternoon and continues on until daylight the next day.

I have gone to many "sing-sings." It is true that one can feel the evil that is involved in the worship part of the event. Everything that is done during these festivals involves the placation of ancestral and other spirits. Fertility rites are also carried on at this time. These rites are to ensure that many children will be added to their tribe during the year, especially male children.

A major problem that we had in presenting the gospel was relating God to their particular needs.

One of those needs was the necessity to find a way to make themselves right or righteous with the spirit world. This included ancestral spirits and the spirits of the jungle. The Kobons seemed to be continually in conflict with the spirit world. They seem to feel that every year or so they had to make a big sacrifice with smaller ones between times. A blood sacrifice always seemed to be the supreme sacrifice; sweet potatoes, corn, sugar cane, pitpit, taro, and kumu are never enough.

My children, Susan and Daryl, Jr., who I might say have been a great help in understanding the customs of our people, had helped a friend finish his small garden. Upon completion of the garden he asked if they would like to eat some food with him at the edge of his garden. They thought this was a good idea so they said they would. He then produced a little bird which he had killed and proceeded to cook with sweet potatoes. Our children quickly realized that this wasn't just a cookout, but that it had a spiritual significance. Upon realizing this they refused to participate. There again a blood sacrifice was important if the garden was to grow well.

When we were constructing the Dusin airstrip, I found out that as the men turned over the ground and began moving it to other places, they cut their tongues with bamboo and spit the blood onto the spaded ground. I discovered they did this so that the spirits would not harm them for scarring the surface of the ancestral ground.

I struck on the idea that our people here, though corrupted by Satan and very primitive, believed very similarly to concepts described in the Scriptures; their

*Beginning of the Dusin church, Daryl Schendel leading the service.*

teaching that a blood sacrifice is necessary for the atonement of sin had its direct parallel in the Old Testament. I began preaching on the subject that Jesus, the Supreme Sacrifice, had shed His blood and that there is no need for shedding of more blood. All we have to do is take advantage of His blood for the cleansing of our sins, and to become righteous in the sight of the true and living God.

The church began to grow among the Kobons, and we give God all the praise for these are His people and the sheep of His pasture. He is their Shepherd, and He cares for them. It has not been easy for them to turn from their evil ways, for much of their culture is permeated with ancestral and evil spirit worship.

Elizabeth, being a registered nurse and also having a degree in elementary education, had her work cut out for her. Among the Kobon people nothing had ever been done in medicine or education.

The Kobon people have always had their own traditional kind of medicine that involved the ancestor spirits and the "poison man." If the sickness was small they usually didn't call the important "poison man," for he is too expensive. His services are usually paid for by a pig and some shells.

One day while I was building our workshop at Salemp, I observed a very interesting happening. An older man with a cold and sore throat was coughing. A young man came over to him and put one hand on his chest and the other hand on his back and rubbed his hands upward with a jerk. After doing this three or four times and chanting some words which I was unable to understand, he stooped down and picked up a small rock off the ground. The practitioner explained that he had gotten the rock out of this sick man's throat, and that he would be alright now.

When we first arrived the people were not sure about the white man's medicine. Many would not come to the clinic. But after a while, whey they began to see that those who did come and got medicine were getting well, they were less afraid. It was really amazing to see penicillin work. The people here had never had medicine before in their lives, so one injection of penicillin seemed to work miracles. Also antimalarial medicine was a miracle worker. The main kinds of illness are pneumonia, malaria, and tropical ulcers.

Elizabeth set up a clinic immediately off our back porch, while the bush house clinic was under construction. It had woven bamboo floors, woven reed walls, and a grass roof. The frame was made of round poles. Elizabeth moved in before we had it completed, for the people began to want more of her time and medicine.

She immediately started to train a "dokta boi" to treat minor illnesses and injuries and to call her when someone came in with a more serious illness. Many times we would go out into the bush to give medicine to people too sick to be carried into the clinic. I had never given an injection, but a missionary does a lot of things he has never had to do before. I remember going out to sick people; praying for them and giving them an injection of penicillin along with some antimalaria tablets.

I well remember one experience in particular. We had been given an urgent message that a local government official (the "Luluai") at Wulim village was very sick and thought he was going to die. Elizabeth and I got on the Honda 175 and headed out over a rough mountain trail to find the "Luluai." After a 45-minute ride we left the bike and slid down through the bush, in the mud and muck. We heard a lot of noise, chanting and yelling, so we moved through the jungle trying to see what was going on, peering through the reeds and underbrush.

Arriving on the scene we found that a large pig had been killed and was in the "mumu" cooking. The "poison man" was making a lot of commotion. When he saw us he stopped and came over and shook our hands and said he still had some more ritual to go through but it shouldn't be too long now. We said we would wait and he carried on with his ritual of exorcising of the ancestral spirits or evil spirits.

He grabbed up tree branches and started pounding the ground with them. While yelling, he brushed off the "Luluai" to get the evil spirits out of him. The "Luluai" was filthy with ashes and dirt which had been used to exorcise the evil spirit.

Upon completion of the ritual we gave the government representative a shot of penicillin, some aspirin, and antimalaria tablets. Then I had a word of prayer asking God not only to heal but to save this man.

The next day I went to him again with an injection, some medicine, and the power of the Holy Spirit. Today both the "poison man" and the "Luluai" are growing Christians with an exciting testimony of sins forgiven.

They are our leaders in the Church of the Nazarene at Wulim. Praise God!

The medical program has been a real area of service to our people. We have young New Guineans doing the medical work today.

One of the strongest means of evangelism has come through our Pidgin English literacy program. It was aimed primarily at children and teenagers. Elizabeth started a school as soon as we arrived at Salemp. Today we are seeing the fruit of this early ministry. The main purpose of the literacy program was to get Kobon kids saved and grounded in the Christian faith, while at the same time they were becoming literate.

Our ultimate goal was that some of these young people would be called into the pastoral ministry and go to our Bible college at Ningei in the Waghi Valley. A number of them did attend the school. Some of the children from the early classes have graduated from our Bible col-

*School days as the Dusin literacy program gets underway*

lege and are pastors to their own people. Others are students in the Bible college studying and preparing to go into the pastoral ministry.

It is always a red-letter day on any mission field when the church appoints a pastor from the ranks of the country's own young people. Traditionally, these persons are called national pastors. But the word "national" doesn't do justice to the importance of persons of like origins, ministering to their own people. Missionary pastors are only stopgap arrangements.

The Kobon people received James Yekip, their first New Guinean pastor, in September, 1970. He was appointed by then Field Superintendent Rev. Lee Eby. A graduate of Nazarene Bible College in Waghi Valley, Yekip accepted a call to preach while working as a laborer in the Kudjip hospital. He enrolled in Bible college in 1968.

While a student, Pastor Yekip heard veteran missionary Prescott Beals speak in chapel. One message compared the stages of full salvation to three jars of water: The muddy water was one's life containing unconfessed sin; the jar of clear water with pebbles, that were easily stirred up, represented the saved but unsanctified life; finally, the third jar was of pure water and was easily understood to be the sanctified life. This simple object lesson message spoke to James Yekip's heart. He responded to the invitation for cleansing. His life has shown a stability and depth that comes only from the Holy Spirit.

The young minister arrived at his charge in Salemp and began his ministry with enthusiasm and godly strength. His ministry there has been neither easy nor without problems, but God has made Pastor Yekip a man with leadership capabilities. Yekip has seen the Church of the Nazarene grow among the Kobons from 1 to 12

*Pastor James Yekip; his wife, Janie; and children Susan and Kathryn.*

churches and preaching points. There are many more in sight for the near future. The growth has been due largely to his Spirit-directed leadership. He has been God's man for the hour. We see great things ahead in his ministry.

Pastor Yekip is not a man from the Kobon area. Coming from Pangia in the Southern Highland Province, he did not know the Kobon customs and language. Because his home area had been reached by civilization and the gospel only a few years before his conversion, Yekip's background was what is considered heathen. But God had a special work for him in His kingdom. Pastor James Yekip's future looks bright and exciting as he follows Christ and works for Him through the Church of the Nazarene.

Pastor Yekip is married and has three children. His wife, Janie, is a strong Christian and has been a real help to him. The children are Susan, age five; Susana, age three; and Kathryn, age one. Susana is an adopted daughter who has an interesting story.

A couple of years ago in the Gebra Valley, Susana's father had shot a wild pig with a bow and arrow. The animal was not killed instantly, only wounded.

On this particular occasion Susana's mother was tracking the wounded pig, which unnoticed had circled around and then attacked Susana's mother from behind. It knocked her down to the ground and with its long tusks tore her legs and ripped open her abdomen. By the time help could get to her, she had bled to death.

Pastor Yekip and Janie took Susana to their home, for there was no one in the immediate family who wanted her or was able to take care of her.

Pastor Yekip's family is a real credit to him and the Church of the Nazarene. We here in Papua New Guinea are proud to have a pastor and family such as this one on our staff.

# 5

# A Perch for the Big Yellow Bird

When we moved into Salemp, in January, 1970, I continued to look for an airstrip site somewhere in the Kairongk Valley. We needed an easier access than the 20-mile bush trail that the family had to travel to get in and out of the Kobon area.

Every couple of weeks I would go with my tape measure to check out what various people would describe as a perfect place for an airstrip. Almost all of the locations I checked out were only large enough to accommodate a helicopter pad.

One day late in 1970 a young man came up to me and said, *Masta Schendel, mi save long gutpela ples long putim ples balus* ("Mister Schendel, I know of a good place you can build an airstrip"). I said to myself, "Oh, no, not another wild goose chase." But because I was anxious to check out every possibility, we went on a long day's trek to find this perfect piece of ground he knew about.

We hiked straight down to a river about 45 minutes from the mission, and then straight up the other side about twice as high as from where we had started. There were no roads, just some bush trails. Arriving at the suggested spot we could see practically nothing. We had to pick our way through the thick jungle growth where only pigs and rodents lived. We were in mud up to our knees and could see only 3 feet on either side.

As we walked and crawled along I became more and more excited, for the ground seemed quite level, at least what I could see of it. There were huge trees covering most of the area. I prayed, "Lord, could this be what we have been looking for?" In a very short time I felt the answer was Yes.

We rounded up about 15 men that day to cut away and push down the bush. We cleared a swath 30 feet wide down the middle of what I thought could be airstrip. When we pushed aside as much of the bush as possible, I used the tape measure and could measure out only 600 feet. That's wasn't even half enough space for the landing strip, but the jungle was so thick up on the far end that it was impossible to measure. I could tell that the next 800 feet was going to be a miracle.

I sat down that day with the men who were with me and told them that I believed we had an airstrip site in the making. I explained that the job was going to be gigantic and that if they would clear all the jungle bush and trees and burn the debris, I would give them a case of mackerel fish and a 50-pound bag of rice. That was all they needed. The word went out far and wide that the Church of the Nazarene was going to build an airstrip at what is now known as Dusin.

The weeks that followed were busy for the local people at the landing strip site. From our home at Salemp I could see smoke rising from the proposed "airport." Through binoculars I saw more and more jungle turning brown and then the bare ground began to show.

One day a group of men came and said they were ready for the payment of fish and rice I had promised.

**60**

They wanted me to come and measure the ground. As I looked at the cleared strip my faith was a bit shaken. There was no problem with the first 600 feet that I measured, but at the 700-800-foot mark there was a mountain extending out into the middle of the proposed site. The balance of the strip was problematic too. I knew the situation could be rectified with a bulldozer, but with hands and shovels it was an almost impossible task.

I tried to explain to the men what kind of a task it was going to be. I told them it was almost impossible, but they kept assuring me that they would be able to do it. I explained that I would need to do more study and that I was willing to try it if they were.

In November, 1970, I had a serious illness that necessitated a helicopter to take me out to the Kudjip Hospital. We took this opportunity to bring in an engineer to survey the proposed airstrip site. He did the survey that day before I left and submitted a report of what he felt it would take to complete the airstrip on that piece of ground. His report was another blow to my faith. I almost gave up the idea of building this airstrip in this particular location.

The engineer said it was possible to build the airstrip, but not probable. His recommendation was, "Don't try it." He advised that it would take us three years and $15,000. Without a bulldozer we had "bitten off" a difficult job.

We prayed and thought about our project for several months. We than gathered several hundred of the local people together to discuss the job that was ahead of us. They would not be able to do the job without me and I would not be able to do it without them, so together we agreed to tackle the almost impossible project.

Time came for us to furlough and to try to raise money for the airstrip construction. We went home knowing that upon our return there was a very difficult job waiting for us.

Upon our return from furlough, July, 1972, we began preparing to move our home to the airstrip site. The local people gave us a small piece of ground on which to build temporary housing.

In the months that followed I had the ground cleared and a small grass-roof house constructed. This house would serve as our living room, kitchen, and classroom for the kids who were being taught by correspondence.

Nearby we erected a metal-roof shed with no walls that was later to protect our 14-foot sleeping tent from the heavy downpours and scorching tropical sun. This metal roof would also provide a means for catching our water supply.

We built another small building with a grass roof, dirt floor, and reed walls that would serve as our bathroom. I was able to rig up a regular flush toilet. We used a large bucket for showering. I also used this small room for a darkroom when I found some spare time for my photography hobby.

The Schendel family moved from Salemp to the Dusin hut and tent in November of 1972. This was to be our home for the next eight months. I've always enjoyed camping, but eight months of it was a bit difficult. These situations provide times when one finds out whether his committment is really what it ought to be. Our kids never complained or questioned; neither did Elizabeth.

November, 1972, we began the airstrip job that we felt God wanted done. I felt with all my heart that we

*Building the Dusin airstrip by hand. Note the gunnysack stretchers in which the dirt was carried. Below, the completed runway as seen from the air.*

could build this airstrip, but I never dreamed that with our 20 workers mountains could be moved and valleys made straight in such a short time.

We gave some of the men shovels and the others gunnysacks which were fashioned into stretchers. The workers with the shovels scooped up the earth and tossed it onto the stretchers. The two stretcher bearers carried their load of dirt to the fill spot and dumped it. Wheelbarrows were very difficult for our people to handle. The had trouble balancing the load weight on one wheel. Also, the wheelbarrows were made for people with long legs. Most of our Kobon men were not more than 5 feet 4 inches tall. When our people lifted up on the handles, they either had to walk on their toes or cradle the handles in the crook of their elbows.

Day after day we worked. Manpower grew, which gave me a difficult time keeping up with them. I had to be on the site at all times so the crew would know where to cut and where to fill. I decided to put stakes at each corner of 10 foot squares, which they would either fill or use to measure areas that needed to be cut.

Along with the construction of the airstrip, I had to build a workshop of bush and grass material to store all the airstrip equipment and supplies. A missionary residence also had to be completed. Then too, the churches had to be supervised. New pastors were arriving regularly to take up their pastorates. With all these projects going on at the same time, the months moved by very rapidly.

In January and February, 1973, the work force increased to 190, which was quite a crew to supervise. But many hands and feet made the work move rather quickly. I do remember one day standing at the lower end of the airstrip and saying, "Lord, if only You would perform a miracle, it could all be finished in the morning." But it didn't happen quite that rapidly.

Some interesting events took place while the strip was under construction. In February of 1973, we decided to have MAF and Rev. Ray Bolerjack do a supplies air-drop. The people were excited and worried about the plane coming. They thought it was going to try to land on the unfinished airstrip. As the plane made its last pass and all the cargo had been dropped on the airstrip, we all rushed out to look into the bags. Among other things, we had had Rev. Bolerjack deliver $600 worth of 10 cent pieces. When they hit the ground, the money burst out of the paper wrappers and was loose inside the canvas cargo bag. When the people looked inside the bag and saw the money, they naturally thought God had answered their prayers and sent them money out of heaven. We tried to explain that it had come from the bank in Mount Hagen, but they all knew better than that.

The local Kobon women were never allowed on the surface of the airstrip. The men who were working believed that if the women walked across it the project would never be finished. Also, as was stated earlier, the men would periodically cut their tongues and spit the blood on the surface.

Heavy rains in January, February, and March made work very difficult. I suppose the downpours facilitated the packing of the fill areas, but it made working conditions very muddy.

The months of hard labor and long hours continued until May 17, 1973, when the airstrip was officially opened. MAF was asked to make the initial landing, signifying that it was officially open.

This opening was one of the most exciting days of our lives for this was the day that the first "balus" or plane would land in this edge of nowhere region. Twelve hundred people gathered to see the "yellow bird" make its first landing. It was a day of great joy, because so many people had worked so very hard to see this event come to pass.

Everything for the celebration was ready, and we waited. People lined the airstrip. They sat on the mountainside overlooking the strip. I recall standing there with the rest of the crowd, straining to hear the airplane engines. When I finally heard the first drone of a Cessna 185 headed for Dusin, my heart leaped into my throat. We watched pilot Dave Grace of MAF make his circuit and head down for a final approach with flaps down. I could do nothing but praise God for the miracle airstrip at Dusin.

Pilot Grace touched down the "yellow bird" on the runway very nicely and taxied into the parking bay. We all converged around the aircraft. Many of the people, hav-

*The first landing at Dusin*

ing never seen or been near an airplane, had to touch the plane to see if it were warm- or cold-blooded. They wanted to know if it was really a bird or not. Pictures were taken of the first cargo to arrive at Dusin airport. In the custom of Papua New Guinea, we prepared a feast of celebration. We had a dedication service which included MAF, the Government Patrol Officer, Mission Directors Wallace and Mona White, all the local tribal leaders of the area, myself and family. To the five men who had originally owned the ground which is now the airstrip and mission station, we gave fish and rice as a token of appreciation.

An airstrip, 1,500 feet long, 100 feet wide, on an 11 percent grade, carved out of a mountain, became a reality because of the prayers and giving of Nazarenes around the world, the financial contributions of the Harold Moran family, and the hard work of the Kobon people.

Dusin airstrip is a dedicated instrument to be used in reaching the Kobon people with the gospel.

# 6

# New Faces
# and a Downed Bomber

Soon after moving to Salemp we learned of more people who had not yet been contacted with the gospel. They lived about four days' walk from where we lived. At this time I had been having men's prayer meetings, and had been visiting with the local men around their fires trying to pick up the language and become better acquainted. Around these fires I heard about a large airplane that had crashed many years before. I tried to find out if it was a small plane like the Cessna 185 or was it much larger?

None of the local men had actually seen it because it was so far out in the bush, but they did know of a man who had actually seen the plane. I told them that I would like to talk to the man as soon as possible. Several days later a man showed up saying he had actually seen the crashed plane and he thought it had two large objects on each side of a big tube-like house. One thing he did know for sure, the plane was bigger than the Cessna 185 he had seen at the Simbai airstrip. We talked for a while and found out that it was in the same general area where I had planned my next patrol.

We set the patrol for July 21-31, 1970, and notified the government patrol officer that we were going into this very primitive area. We also explained that we had heard stories of a crashed plane in that area and we thought we would check it out. The patrol officer gave his permission and we began to make definite plans.

Dr. Paul Chiles, who was helping at the Kudjip hospital during this time, decided to go with me to do some medical work among the primitive people that we planned to contact.

When July 21 came we had our cargo ready; the carriers were on hand, and we left civilization (our Salemp mission home) for a place we knew nothing about. We were excited about getting out again into the jungle and reaching people who had never heard the gospel story.

The first day out always seems to be the hardest day on leg muscles. Because of the mountainous terrain, our pace was slowed to the point where we were unable to reach the Sangapi rest house before dark. We were forced to make camp along the trail. Pitching our tent, we hoped that it wouldn't rain very hard, for our tent wasn't completely waterproof. But rain it did. As the tent became saturated, it began to fill up with water. By morning there were at least three inches sloshing around us. We were glad to see the sun come up the next morning as we took off on our way again. Our carriers had spent the night all along the trail in little lean-to huts made out of bush material. Being unable to sleep on the ground because of the rain running through, they slept on their haunches. A most difficult thing for most of us to do.

After a couple more hours of walking in the bright sunlight, we were able to set up camp at Sangapi rest house. We decided to spend a couple of nights there before going on. It was an enjoyable time visiting again with the people of Sangapi. We had a well attended church service. I had a lot of memories centered around Sangapi, for it was here we were going to live originally; we have a number of friends in that settlement.

We left Sangapi for Aradip, where we spent the night. Altitude at that spot is around 6,500 feet, which makes it quite cool. It always seems like the winds are stronger up there. There were quite a few people in Aradip, and because it was another language group, we had to speak to them through two interpreters.

The next morning we moved into the primary area of interest for this patrol. We climbed over a large mountain range and dropped into the narrow valley below. The rain forest was so thick that it was impossible to see the sky. The tropical flowers and birds were everywhere,

*Wreckage of a World War II A20G Douglas fighter-bomber discovered after 28 years*

and the calls of the magnificent birds of paradise were heard from the tops of the trees where they stay.

Arriving on the valley floor, we found two or three houses but very few people. There did not seem to be as many as we had anticipated. So we set up our tent at what is now known as "Schendel's Bluff" and prayed that it would not rain. The carriers built some lean-to huts. We had church with the carriers and what few local people we could find.

It was in this area that we had heard that the crashed plane was located so we left camp early in the morning with no cargo and climbed straight up the other side of the valley. There were no trails, so we had to pick our way up and through the thick foliage. Many times we found it necessary to retrace our route for another, or climb over giant boulders and fallen trees.

Our five-hour hike came to an end at a mountain ridge. I have no idea of the altitude, but it was very cold. Some of our men claimed we were close to the downed airplane. My excitement was mounting.

From the vantage point of the ridge we were able to make out the form of what turned out to be the wing of an airplane. Just opposite the wing, a short distance away, we saw the fuselage and other wing. The main body of the aircraft was overgrown with jungle vines and bush. When I discovered the large U.S.A. star insignia, my excitement rose even higher. Here was an American World War II fighter-bomber, we later learned, that had become lost from the rest of the squadron, and crashed into the ridge. Our New Guinean carriers were not interested in risking evil spirits by coming any closer to the airplane. Thus it was with all who passed by that spot. Consequently, everything remained just as when the tragedy took place.

Dr. Paul and I approached the aircraft, which was resting upside down. We took photographs, investigated the outside of the plane, and then turned our attention to the interior. In the back portion of the cabin we discovered the remains of two crew members, a photographer and a gunner. They were probably just where they had fallen on that day in March, 1943. Their dog tags were not to be found. In the cockpit area, however, we did find a set of dog tags; they belonged to pilot Allen Garlick. This portion of the plane must have burned upon impact.

Just to the rear of the aircraft I found a live bomb cradled in the "arms" of a tree root. Large 50-caliber machine guns with dozens of cartridges were lying around the area.

The U.S. government has filled in the details of this war story. They report the Douglas A20G fighter-bomber had left Nadzab military airstrip near the town of Lae for a bombing run not too far from the town of Wewak in March, 1943. Upon return the crew proceeded up the wrong valley. When engine troubles developed and then realizing where they were, the crew tried to fly the plane over the Bismark Schrader Range, but weren't able to clear the ridge. The local people had stories of their own that it had come from the spirit world. We secured all the information needed and headed down the mountain to camp. It was a thrilling experience for us to be the ones to discover the remains of three American servicemen who had been missing in action for 28 years.

The conclusion to this event took place in 1971 while we were on furlough. It was our privilege to visit with the pilot's mother and father in Bloomington, Minn. This was a particular high point of our first furlough. God is good and gives us many blessings that we neither ask for nor deserve.

Continuing our patrol, we returned to Sangapi and then crossed another ridge of mountains to the beautiful Gebra Valley. From there we returned home to Salemp. We never cease to thank God for His protection on these patrols into unexplored areas.

Our trip heightened concern for the Gebra Valley and the more than 1,000 people living there. Pastor Yekip felt such deep concern that he decided to start a church there. It was a six-hour walk from Salemp to Gebra Valley but Yekip felt the people there must hear of Jesus Christ before it was too late. He would go every two or three weeks and hold a church service in the valley. James Sambal, a Christian layman from Salemp church, built Gebra Valley's first church building out of local bush materials in 1970.

In 1973, Pastor John Kol Kina (Kee-na), his wife and son, were assigned to the Gebra church. At this time we built another church building out of local bush materials and a pastor's residence which was semipermanent (corrugated iron roof with reed walls). The first baptismal service was in 1975 and the church has been growing steadily ever since. From zero to 25 members in five years. This is good growth when one considers how far they have come.

The Wulim Church of the Nazarene was started in 1973 by Pastor Yekip and within a few months another pastor was assigned there, Samson Maki Pu (Poo). Pastor Maki came to Wulim just out of Bible college and began building a parsonage, a church, and a school building by himself out of local building materials. Within a year or so people started finding the Lord. Two government officials were saved along with a young man by the name of Alangin (A-*lan*-jun). Since 1976, when Pastor Maki Pu was transferred, Alangin has taken over leadership as a lay pastor. Alangin, who is a local man, has been able to preach to his people through his own language where both previous pastors had to speak through an interpreter. The Wulim church now has about 20 members and is a growing church.

Hangable (Hang-ga-ble) village sent people up to Dusin, wanting us to come so that they too could hear the gospel story. Pastor Yekip, not having someone to send, decided to go himself as often as possible. He built a church building in which to worship. In 1975 the Church of the Nazarene was able to send Pastor and Mrs. Bare (Ba-re) and family to minister in Hangable, where the church is located at 3,000 feet above sea level. The temperature is very warm and the people there are more sickly than in other Kobon areas. Hangable is located about a five-hour walk from our Dusin mission station. After two years of ministering, Pastor Bare baptized 12 Christians. Pastor Maban of the local language group and a 1977 graduate of our Nazarene Bible College, has been assigned to Hangable.

Sangapi Village, once going to be our first area of evangelism, became one of our last. The population in the valley is quite sparse but in 1976 we were able to shift Pastor Maki Pu to pioneer the work there. The Sangapi people are some of the most primitive, but Pastor Maki has been instrumental in winning a number to Christ.

The pastor tells about one Sunday morning when a storm came up and a bolt of lightening struck the church just as everyone had moved out. The bolt traveled down a wooden rafter, making it charcoal, and across the ground where it struck one of the Christian women, knocking her unconscious. The people thought she was dead. Everyone was frightened, but the pastor gathered the other Christians around and prayed until she regained consciousness. This was a very exciting experience for these primitive people. Today there are 20 to 30

74

Christians and each Sunday the church is full of worshipers.

In 1975 Rev. Don Walker and I planned a 10-day contact patrol. I needed to explore an area of the Schrader Range I had never been in before. It is always rewarding to go into untouched areas to preach.

After two days of walking through the Gebra Valley, we topped a ridge and looked over into the Hamil (*Ha*-meel) Valley. What a breathtaking view! We could see all the way down to the Ramu River, 40 to 50 miles away, snaking its way to the sea. The valley isn't heavily populated, but those who are there are *the* most primitive of all our Kobon people. They have had virtually no contact with the outside world. As we walked on down the trail into Gaimbaum Village our hearts went out to the people who met us. We had to get a church started as soon as possible. The church has been started at Gaimbaum (*Gaeem*-bam) Village, with a layman going every Sunday to hold services. The pastor at the Gebra church

*Kobon people hearing the gospel for the first time at Gaimbaum village.*

75

gives him his message and he delivers it to the Gaimbaum congregation. We are praying that we will be able to send a full-time pastor to Gaimbaum very soon.

As we walked on down the valley from Gaimbaum Village we came upon a very different sort of people. The men wore only a small net in front which hung from a reed belt. They wore nothing on the back. Even our carriers were surprised that these people were that primitive. The women's skirts were very similar to the rest of the Kobon women.

The "Tul-tul" in the area thought we were the government patrol officers and came out in all his finery—a shirt, part of a pair of trousers, and a hat. When he found out we were missionaries he appeared next with a pair of trousers, then later just his belt and netting.

We held a church service and people seemed to enjoy it. They had little idea what it was all about, but they participated in everything but closing their eyes for prayer.

As far as we know we have made contact with all the tribes in the Kobon area. It is true we've not been able to send full-time pastors to minister to them all, but we have young Kobon men in training at our Bible college that we are praying will be called by God to go back and preach to their own people.

# 7

# Challenge for the Future

As my family and I approached the time for our second furlough in May of 1976, we began to look back at all the things that had happened since we started construction on our first building at Salemp in 1969. We could only give God the praise for the miracles that had been brought about in our lives, as well as in the lives of our Kobon people whom we had come to serve.

We remembered the first baptismal class in August of 1972, when James Sambal, Giju (Gee-joo), and Timothy Gaimp (Gaeemp), were baptized. These men are still serving God and are very active in their local churches.

The continual conversions, baptismal services, and churches organized were true miracles of God's grace. Changed hearts and lives were evident. Where previously there were killings and tribal wars, we have seen the peace of God prevail. Not all the Kobon people are Christians by any means, but God's love has invaded their culture.

A young man from Dusin Village told me this story before we left on furlough. It was late afternoon when he

*Wallace White and Daryl Schendel baptize Giju, the first Kobon Christian.*

heard that some at Wulim Village, about four miles away, had insulted him and his tribe. He was so angry that he started off to Wulim to find this man and kill him with a razor sharp axe (our people very seldom fight with their fists, they always fight to kill). On his way to the village he began to feel that this was something he ought not to do. He said since the mission had come with "God's talk," this kind of fighting should be done away with. So he changed his walking direction and came to talk to me about it. God does indeed influence even the most primitive to do good.

The national pastors had been taking a more active role in the running of the churches as we approached furlough. Pastor Yekip was becoming a stronger leader, and our responsibility as missionaries became more supportive than initiating. We do admit that this was a very frustrating role to play but when we saw how God was using these men, how the church was growing, and that people were being converted with less and less of our help, it became a very satisfying experience.

As we left Papua New Guinea for furlough we challenged our pastors to move out for Christ. We told them they must not wait for a missionary, for time is too short. The gospel must be preached to every man, woman, and child.

We did not know when we went on furlough whether our assignment, upon return, would be back among the Kobon people or not. We had prayed that they would be excited and challenged with the prospect of being dependent on the Holy Spirit.

While on furlough we received letters stating how God was blessing with new preaching points and churches. Not once did any pastor say, "We are just waiting till you come back and then we will start work." Baptismal and membership classes, pastors' meetings, camp meetings, NYI meetings, continued to be the pattern of events. Upon our departure from the field it seemed to make no difference, for they were not working for the missionary but for God through the power of the Holy Spirit.

Upon our return from furlough we were given another assignment. But the task of winning men and women to Jesus, planting the Church of the Nazarene in every village and hamlet throughout the "edge of nowhere" continues on.